based on a true story

remember that the root of your hair is every single inch. know thyself.

— tevin dubé

Also By Tevin Curtis Ryan Dubé

Book Of The Enlightened One

Amen: A Great Light Within Divine Darkness

The Mystery Behind Life, Death and Resurrection

A Silent Truth

Psalms From A New King David

S
E
L
F

Tevin C. R. Dubé

ISBN: 978-976-96334-1-4

Publishers Note

Tevin Curtis Ryan Dubé

Trinidad and Tobago

Email: tevindube@yahoo.com

Facebook Page –Tevin 'Mystical' Dube

Instagram – mystical_dube

Twitter – @mysticaldube

Cover Design by Tevin C. R. Dubé

Contents

let me paint a picture-perfect portrait

portrayed completely with words

upon the canvas of your mind

allow my pain to be your healing

as much as your healing

shall be a living testament

to my redemption

self-hate

if i had my way

quite frankly

i would never choose to be

born in this particular flesh

why would any conscientious being

chose to be born

in a vessel detested?

suffering as i imagined myself

with a different face

with preferably a lighter complexion

savoury towards society's bitter taste buds

so many closely knitted

clustered and plastered beyond

my own liking

like a contagious disease

a plague

like the frogs and locusts

unleashed by moses

but equally painful as job's leprosy

this is how i felt

looking at my epidermis

regretting every pigment

self-destructing

my mind's eye was blinded by

my own two eyes

because my own two eyes

were filled with mist

causing me to see myself

through the foggy lenses of society's

post-colonial mentality

mentally handicapped

how can I gain joy by

such a foolish imaginary concept

of seeing myself in a different

identity, looking for similarities

to compare myself

to that which is considered as desirable

to feel any little good about myself

instilled beliefs in a child

is harder to break

as an adult

for when i was seven

i was angrily called

a black ugly monkey

by my father

and i believed it

for more than a decade

da saw the instant impact

as i tore through my favorite t-shirt

crying even more afterwards

inflicting pain upon my fists

as i hammered away

at a full barrel of water

trying to ease the hurt in my heart

with teary eyes, he did apologise

even though i never uttered my forgiveness

our relationship bloomed

"promise me that you will be better than me"

da asked of me

in which i strongly assured him

because i

had already purposed such within my heart

and by the age of nine

father was no longer here

his spirit escaped his prison of flesh

and he flew away

but from that moment on

i realised that everyone else

could no longer be lying

for if my own flesh and blood

could say it

then it was axiomatic

never underestimate the power of words

especially upon a child

i remember those horrid teenage days

when i was afraid to look at my own face

i opted to look in a mirror at night

or through tinted car glasses at day

because the darkness helped

to hide my many present flaws

the abyss within my soul

was drowning and swallowing me whole

a phoenix is one that rises from the ashes

that was burnt

but this sunken place knows no growth

once ashes get immersed in water

it quickly disperses

teary eyes, silently drenched pillows many nights

prayers being offered up

from a brokenly contrite heart

i dare not expose my weaknesses

so, my whole life

i had to be strong

it was a hard fact to accept

that i was stuck for life

with this abomination

how can you strip yourself entirely

to rebuild yourself completely

automatically

while still maintaining the same image

simultaneously?

    –   spirituality

i was fighting within and without

i was never the favorite

i was never someone's first choice

i was embraced by depression

i was used by loneliness

depression itself

wants to be relieved from itself

that's why it chooses someone to be dealt with

loneliness wants to be relieved

from its own loneliness

that's why it isolates someone to embrace it

i just never understood it

my intelligence, my compassionate nature

was linked to my depression

my loneliness helped me

to never want another to experience such

hence i willingly sacrificed my joy

to make another happy

i became a light in another's dark

but was lost in my own

i was scared of moving

because i could no longer see

the fact

that i was the light

in my own dark all along

self-realisation

dressing became my alternative outlet for escape

but i was mostly still a prisoner

freedom is always bitter-sweet

after captivity

i wanted independence

but my humble beginnings never permitted me

i was lacking the means to materialism

at fourteen i wanted to become more of a man

the burdens of my single mother

had long dawned upon me

i saved for months dollar by dollar

to buy one t-shirt

then one pant

then a pair of sneakers

i still have the stretch marks to show

i jeopardised my own well-being as i starved

during school

to kill two birds with one stone

one: to alleviate myself as a burden unto my mother

two: to experience my temporal escape

self-hate has caused a great vacuum

an emptiness of space

an unbridgeable gap

a vacant soul

filled with bones

just like a tomb

i'm alive but feeling dead

like embalmed flesh

missing the gift of life

i'm artificially preserved by pain

and even though i show love

and can feel it coursing through my veins

i am numbed all the same

a fiery cold flame

something got to give

in my temporary escape

the one time i genuinely felt good about myself

the one time i could truly face myself in a mirror

for a little extended period of time

the one time i felt like somebody

i couldn't trust anybody

so, i could not take any compliments properly

only say i'm looking good

before getting a thank you

you would hear i know

it was not done out of arrogance

but it was my way to protect

what little resources i had left

whatever little self-esteem i had remain

i've been dropped faster than lifted

i've been shunned more than hugged

i was becoming too warm

to the constant coldness, i felt

low self-esteem is to be wandering

a lonely wilderness within the soul

almost like a floating balloon

let loose by hands once held

being tossed by the elements

and at any given time can just pop

i still decided to show love

even though i could not afford it for myself

i decided to want to become a beast

but in the end

i literally couldn't breathe

it was my first encounter with death

that changed my mind

but in years to come it once again rearranged

and i was now experiencing death a second time

this time i was certain

that my existence was very much slipping away

because i was being surrounded

by a darkness

only my eyes could perceive

during the prime of the day

where i saw no leaves ruffling

because for weeks i never felt the wind

when out in the open

those nights i was scared to sleep

i felt the setting of my sun

when i was still so young

still learning how to survive

i realised i was re-enacting all that my father had felt

i was present to it all

so now i knew more about how it felt

to be cut off from it all

not even the ones you love could fill that void

he confirmed to me the inevitability of his death

indeed, he did and now i was next

words may be convincing yet untrue

but raw emotions never lie

i chose to do one little thing he never did

i cast whatever little faith i had

upon the steps of the god i knew

and it turned away an impending storm

i mysteriously felt rejuvenated

as i was filled once again with the breath of life

contentious beliefs and in contempt i felt

when i saw blatant contradictions towards myself

look for someone with nice hair and light skin

that way you can have nice children

such came from my kin

i first explored the light in that statement

it was never meant to be malicious

it truly is a tough world for someone like me

and i was plunged

into this pandemonium unprotected

for there is no physical protection

for mental attacks

having a child for society's standards

would save them

they would be spared

from blatant neglect and reject

it would save them

from having to feel the hell i felt

but here comes the dark side of the moon

for i was always a deep thinker

people like myself would go extinct

with such a heinous mantra

if we all were to seek babies

upon the requirements of society

then what would be the purpose of diversity

a nonentity i gradually felt like

yet still i showed a pure love unto many

simply because i always wanted the same

but even though it came from a few

i knew had a genuine love

i felt alone

what if we never had blood relations

i would still very much be an outcast

because i already was towards me

that same day after i was intimately kissed

by the breath of life

i sat before a mirror and confronted myself

i looked deep into my eyes

the strokes within were magnificent

my thick afro i saw was amazing

my natural integument shone darkly

every pigment now twinkled in my eyes

and all my flaws even though still present

was yet still being concealed

by the perfection i saw

beauty is truly in the eyes of the beholder

so, i dug the scales out of mines

and i saw that society was truly blind

when i was being taught otherwise

i fell in love with myself for the very first time

i began to slowly understand

i was made to not see

all which i possessed all along

it was like i said back when i was fourteen

probably the first real-time

i consciously overheard my intuition

many envy you because of what they can see

one day to come you will be doing great things

things that right now you yet cannot see

despite it all, i wore my magic and excelled

i never thought that

i would become a number one

well not in the heart

but atop my entire school

despite all the fight down

prejudice and racism

and financial difficulties

where i worked hard for a year to resend myself

i made my mother cry

my triumphs had to reflect her sacrifices

i gave all my accolades to her

as strangers sang my praises like a choir

yet still i came and fell further into the abyss

but life kissed me passionately

a rebirth

an offspring from precious cargo on ships

ancestors once enslaved

still mentally charred from centuries of disdain

with the same oppression hereditarily gained

infused with unknown royalty all the same

a rare gem shipwrecked

upon a little island

to rise like a phoenix

from the abyss into the tropics

freedom is a must

emancipation means responsibility

liberty requires work

such are the basic requirements

towards the acceptance of self

a poem of depression

inspired by leshon leacock

agonising are these thoughts of mine

this carnal thinking is disturbing my divine

simultaneously, i am both my own friend and foe;

you might see me smile but deep down you may
never know

depression is linked to intellect,

even though i know myself, i still don't know me yet

at nights i cry for my pain to be taken away

in broad daylight, i am still searching for a brighter
day

intense a pain is exactly how it feels,

i am hungry with food and can't eat a single meal

in the presence of water, a thirsty horse is foolish to
never drink

a mind overwhelmed with thoughts and i still cannot think

i have realised that i need to thoroughly love myself;

from negativity, positivity would never be my recompense

daily i will try to live best this life i've gained;

i may not see it now but all living things, still need the rain

self-acceptance

post-colonial stress

mental disorders

no one ever admits we still suffer from

it's like we are not liable to experience such

it's not like we've never been decimated

enduring centuries of unimaginable horrors

then to live through jim crow and the kkk

and now uncle tom's cabin is worldwide

spreading corrupt regimes and totalitarian means

from flawed democracy through political greed

like giving us just the right miseducation we need

to feed the ego of the one percent elites

away from the bright lights

puppeteering

blindness is the new sight

proudly carrying our plantation names as surnames

i guess we have legitimate fake id's

that best represents our truly lost identities

the media will pardon the fair in skin

the straight in hair

but no sympathy for the *niggers*

the low-lives

the savages

the baboons

the mongrels

the three-fifths of a human being

all of them are thieves

all of them are murders

worst yet if they wear locks

but silence those who dare speak up

because the oppressors always want to speak for us

kill them all

the world eggs on

easily upon all social media platforms

where stereotyping never dies

only exalt our faults

and whisper our triumphs

but constantly turn us against ourselves

where the sleeping effortlessly becomes

a product of their environment

where peter is paying for paul

and paul is now paying for all

economical slaves

a tattooed piece of paper

replacing whips, shackles and chains

the entire world capitalising off our backs

yet we still don't support ourselves

but exploitation from our own brothers

no real assistance from many in power

but will uplift a complete stranger

self-hate goes way beyond the common traits

an educated fool will always be a mule

with a yoke around the neck

if not edified initially from having common sense

truthfully it is always good to know

but wisdom is only gained

when you learn to effectively apply it

and through such understanding is gained

and with all three combined

you do inherit the key to existence

which is to simply wake up

and choose to stay awake

they hate me because i'm *"black"*

but soon you'll know i'm not

they hate me because of my skin

but now you know it's because of a rich heritage

buried deep within

knowledge of self was never a world threat

it has always been a universal movement

existing before the beginning of days

even though ahead, it is still behind

even though high, it is yet still low

a marathon is all about endurance

and cannot be compared to a sprint

it's like being lapped twice

for even though one is at the forefront

doesn't necessarily mean first place,

 where it ends is the same place it all begins

crossing the finish line first is not a guaranteed win

now, when i'm told about nice children

i asked what is a nice child and good hair?!

my complexion is heavenly divine

and my hair is the best too

i will love my children

and they will love me more

regardless of what

my little story will always inspire

now i am able to see

why many never wanted a child like me

to be born in the first place

white supremacy has always been geared at

making us see ourselves in the opposite

to that in which we already are

by erasing and taking away

all that we already were

but the true mystery of all things

are forever coursing through our veins

a spiritual dna eternally encoded

just like cold water placed upon pure honey

the honeycomb pattern is revealed

to prove the authenticity

of its genetic memory

the colonisers' mindset

was then transferred to

the entire human race

through the establishment of different ethnicities

everyone wants to create separate identities

for all to look down upon the once enslaved

yet the earth's initial kings and queens

even though royalty flows through our veins

peasants became our name

with such division created racism and segregation

and nationality, and democracy,

religions and political parties

and now the asians and indians and arabs

stand united against africans

allowing for the continuation

of a modern-day plantation system

notwithstanding the fact

that the colonisers never truly loved anyone

not one pigmented man, woman and child

to divide and rule was and is their whole plan

when it was long proven that we are one

so, we now pour our magic out

to make fertile the barren lands

through blood, sweat and tears

stripping ourselves of the ever-rich motherland

trying to enter a fake promised land

where you need visas as permission

and still, be questioned extensively through customs

but the slave masters continue to enter freely

making a mockery of us

as we continue to make a mockery of ourselves

drinking from the cup of confusion

when asked what is my type

i now respond

my type is someone loyal

someone who possesses divine qualities

through simplicity

a woman that is in tune with herself

always willing to learn and grow

always contented but never settles

someone that would love me for me

and vice versa indeed

because each day i keep accepting myself

the more i come to know myself

the greatest relationship to establish

is one with yourself

yet it is the most difficult

this mind can be your worst enemy

or can be your best friend

there is a great difference

between being alone and feeling lonely

for there is great power to be gained

from learning to spend time with and by yourself

neither of us belong to another

even though many of us are connected

for we all yet still roam different paths

a true relationship with another

is where both parties conscientiously choose

to support each other on their respective journey

to walk alongside each other

to always show love and appreciation

and support till the very end

becoming

the eye of each other's storm

the toils of life are already tough

each is now an escape

a safe place for thoughts

establishing universal confidentiality

but until then

it must first be established

with and within yourself

self-actualisation

pure consciousness is all-knowing

and all-knowing

is the truest form

of supreme consciousness

i was unconsciously conscious as a fetus

to first become consciously unconscious

as a child

but to develop myself

to become consciously conscious

and so too were you

all of this is a test

to make approve

that pure consciousness will eternally be pure

it cannot be tainted

by any amount of physical trauma

it will always be purified within itself

nothing can ever make it lacklustre

for the solution to every problem

lies at the very source of the problem itself

purely formed within heaven

yet still contained within a living tomb

cosmic dust gathered to form this flesh

creation after creation

encased by the triple darkness of space

within the womb

So, as damian marley asked

"are we born all-knowing

or are we born knowing all?"

creation exists within creation

the same way trillions of cells exist within us

is in the same manner we exist within the earth

and even though there are billions of stars

existing within our galaxy

is in the same proportion protons exists

within our brain

there are many seas of men

swimming as semen

within men

there is a lifetime supply of eggs

within women

to eternally give birth infinitely

and within each egg and sperm

infinity exists within itself infinitely

indeed, i was born not knowing my strength

but to only come to know about such

i realised that i could never believe in magic

if i cannot even believe in myself

i was never truly that in which i believed i was

and i was already that in which i never believed

i could never be

a mere mortal instrument of flesh indeed

yet still the embodiment of divinity

such are we

i closed my lips

because the voice of intuition had a better sound

its words were consistently immaculate

it always came with impeccable timing

it is self-activated

but yet still answers upon requests sublime

an internal consultant

a built-in modulator

an auto-correct function

a universal simulator

an internal mystical decoder

the ultimate internal human processing software

the blueprint of thoughts and divine inspiration

invisibility and invincibility

it can only be found and seen initially internally

through fickle flesh

that can yet still establish it visually

as a general idea for all physically

i began to see how perfect

and perfectly aligned the universe is

i saw the connection of all things to it

and generally, coincidence was ruled out

with immediate effect

in my mind for good

in that, i no longer believed in such nonsense

as a young boy, i recognised

how my hair origins had a spiral

just like a hurricane

but to later only realise

that it patterns after the cosmos

the spiralling of an entire galaxy

take a close look at your fingertips

the fine prints can even be found

within the patterns of your fingerprints

but just like space

my hair grows to defy gravity

standing tall because of its strong negative charge

antennas if you may

magnifying universal reception

decoding sunshine

through symmetrical lines

to flow in unison through the spine

nature's crown

the same manner the earth consists of water

so too does this body in the same exactitude

oil and gas are the blood of the earth

the same way we possess such

for they are the containment of life naturally

just like the dark quartz of the earth

there is gold within my skin

yet there is still copper deep within

just like iron ore is found within the earth

the building blocks of our muscles reflect such

for even our skin creates muck-like dirt

with more than sixty miles of vessels

to be found within this frame

a microcosm earth and the universe

i saw myself in possession of an entire kingdom

trillions of beings in cell form are subjected to me

they respond to my every thought

and whatever i may choose to eat

a royalty inherited naturally

a royalty endowed by the force of nature itself

sun rays create a bright glow in the earth

but could never light up space

it is yet still a blinding light

unto the human eyes

the heavens are clouded by a blue continuum

hiding all things in plain sight

is this hue of the blue spectrum

the light of the night is more revealing

than the darkness of the day

perceived as light

because the stellar orders

are clearly visible at night

even though it appears dark to man

but such is the great light

we see but are still blinded unto

these once-considered closely knitted plagues

i found out to be the same content as space

carbon it is in its truest form

the only thing to have existed

but has never yet been born

a gas that can be liquefied and crystallised

solidified and materialised

and decided to come into flesh

a mysterious dark matter transformation

the origins of magic

the same plague is working

in my favour when it was considered heinous

a blessing in disguise

how wrong is mankind's perception?

to get secondary colours

primary ones must first be mixed

the more you combine

the darker the overall hue appears

it is everything besides "black"

this is what our skin represents

it is what we reflect

for it is our universal reflection

it is so bright

that it appears dark to the naked eyes

coloured brightly spiritually

but shone darkly physically

just leave earth's ionosphere

to escape the tricks of sun rays

and you'll see the heavens

eternally contain the same

the mysteries of space

is that it is

the brightest light

it is the greatest evidence

that not everything you see

is what it appears to be

during the human night

it is yet another day

for the spirit to awake to go and play

but during the human day

the spirit gets involuntarily voluntary

we may perceive our sleeping quests as dreams

but in fact, it is an alternate reality

one that isn't governed by time

and is way beyond the flesh

even though connected to the flesh

for the brain is a great link

that bridges spirituality to humanity

therefore, he who can see will see

that the all-seeing eye

is always supreme

now think about reversed psychology

in comparison to that of slavery

through envy and jealousy

we were made to accept all that we are not

because of our genuine love and hospitality

for how can you be "black"

when you are the embodiment of light

many run to get sun tan

to mimic our detested pigmentation

the same age-defying agent

with a natural gloss

in that, you need not make up

botox to get our same thick lips

plastic surgery for bigger buttocks and hips

nappy you will still call your hair

to go straighten it

but hair extensions are to otherwise make thick

because i can't have what you have

i'll make you regret you ever had it

it's all a mental trick

just awake from it

by simply accepting it

these hues are like a coat on the skin

these pigments are similar to chlorophyll

because it eats the sun

just like leaves during photosynthesis

internally making its food

internally we transmute it into vitamin d

these hues are a covering on the skin

commonly called melanin

this is our protection from increasing rays

just like the earth has its magnetic covering

just like the ozone layer

towards the sun

the hue of its halo also appears dark

my sweat is like the precipitation process

but the natural sodium content

causes the liquid to taste like the sea

a combination of all things

still resides within little me

we are all one

for me is still we

and we shall always be

energy eternal and eternal energy

carbon for an eternity

self-love

even though the words black ugly monkey

cut me deeper than a sword

i love my father even more for it

the mortal part of us never knew

that it was all in accordance with the spirit

i am glad i can continue to strive for excellence

so that i may continuously

fulfil my promise to him

not to be better than

but to uplift and honour him

many claim to love christ

and yet still they hate judas

the night could never coexist without the day

likewise, the day without the night

even judas deserves his praise

a king is never defined by his crown

it is just a symbolic representation

to what has long before already been attained

a natural royalty engrained

betrayal of self is no longer an option

for through self, long may he reign

all those who showed me my flaws

i am more than grateful now

it may have been done out of mortal resent

but has been a spiritual love in disguise

because of it, i found perfection

as i perfected my craft

and naturally, i'm elevated

because of my suppression

humbly, it caused me to become greater

both intentionally and by default

it reached the point where everything

in my life now has true meaning

everything is in perfect alignment

with the natural mystic

that allowed me to discover my purpose in life

the second greatest day in our lives

so that i could attain a rebirth

but the process is continuous

for even though i overstand many things

i'm yet still trying to make sense of it all

for learning is perpetual

self-actualisation is when you begin to take

full control of your destiny

but when you finally begin to take such

into your own two hands

it's like legitimately driving a car for the first time

you must first gain an average

and become familiar with the roads travelled

and that comes from more and more practice

yet you may experience some fender benders

it's like learning how to ride a bike

you must first learn to balance yourself

you may fall and gain some bruises

you have to be cautious yet still endearing

because the most dangerous thing in life

is to always play it safe

and to never be a little intrepid

and even when you begin to master yourself

there is still much more room to fall

no saint is seldom without fault

for even masters still have a lot to be mastered

things do happen

for even ascended masters

are still on a perpetual journey

of continuous elevation

for one's destiny is eternal

the answer remains the same

yet still there are infinite equations

to get to it

sometimes our worst curse

can be our greatest blessings and vice versa

and at times both

but the mind's power becomes absolute

through the powers of perspective critical thinking

it brings about a universal balance

it is the thin line

that sits between

what is considered to be

good and evil

the perfect zone

it is like an elephant in the distance

with the appearance of a tiny ant

but the closer you approach it

the more colossal it becomes

you have the power to see things differently

and construct life into your own creation

and make what you want of it

pressurised carbons create the rarest gems

slavery was the ability to test god mortally

the mortal replicas of god

carbon beings are still being pressurised

the outcome

gems walking in flesh

we keep rising to the occasion

we radiate the sunshine

so many greats have risen

and even though all men fall

the spirits of such keep on elevating

marcus garvey

malcolm x

martin luther king

bob marley

nelson mandela

your wide nostrils aren't ugly

you were made for the tropics

you need to inhale more oxygen

to cool down the brain

your hair is not 'picky' at the back without cause

you cannot overheat your brain stem

you contain a higher concentration of carbon

more than many others

you don't need excessive hair all over your body

to bend to keep you warm

you are already heat-insulated

yet electronically charged

we have already proven our love

the entire world has seen it

history has borne the facts in the fine prints

but we are perceived as foolish because of it

the results

the entire globe flourished

from our blood, sweat and tears

the systems of today

are still being fueled by us

by our stupidity

by our love

we are still fighting to be accepted

by those who insist they don't want to

we would support all others

but would barely support ourselves

we would love our enemies

more than we love ourselves

we would forgive all others

but can barely forgive ourselves

we would appraise all others

but have no gratitude towards ourselves

it's time for our prophets

to have more honour

at home

than abroad

in my estimation, judas deserves his praise

that is why i have never yet beaten

any good friday "bobolee"

early i had foreseen the bigger picture

no matter how small it appeared

all you need to do

is take a step back in reflection

sometimes you have to be like a wisdom tooth

know when it's time to take a backseat

today we have to become saviours

to our own selves

for we cannot even recognise

we have become our very own judases

self-love is an expression of self

for the love of self

to self

which is in existence

existing within many of us

suppressed

dig deep, dig deep, dig deep

to love yourself is not racist

to make others hate themselves

and prevent them from rediscovering

and demonstrating love for self

is a racist agenda

and racism at its pinnacle

but also, a demonstration of fear

and a subconscious battle

that even the oppressors need to heal from

for a lack of spirituality

will always lead to

spiritual sickness

manifesting as low frequencies

transmuted into a lowness of thoughts

   –   white supremacy

a giant is only as tall as it stands

so how tall is one asleep

only a god can establish

heaven in hell

a supreme problem

can only be conquered by a supreme being

and yet still we are the ones

who are facing it all

for centuries

and yet still we rise

slowly

to once again reign supreme

to become masters of our destinies

never through the means of bloodshed

pillage and slavery

slowly but surely

to prove long-suffering

to prove resilience

to prove defiance

to prove opulence

to prove divinity

to prove pure spirituality

because the realist parts of us

was never about race

is not about a religion

was never about a colour

or political affiliations and

or any stupid forms of human segregation

it is about experiencing humanity

and establishing pure spirituality in flesh for

universal love binds us and many know not of it

we have always been an example

for we are the proof

we have proven the fact

that the worst flames

will eventually burn itself out

as much as we could have fought fire with fire

we are the epitome of self-love

but until we begin to show it

to ourselves

we would once again

experience its full bliss

on earth universally

and from all matrices

we all shall truly be set free

through the true practice of love for humanity

therefore, searching for proof and truth

is equivalent to searching for you

even christ professed it

that many shall do far greater things

that was not even possible for him

all you need to do is believe in yourself

to become the greatest is simple

just study the greats that were before you

even marcus garvey professed it

millions more shall rise

and i am but one that yet still consists of

the many that came before me

and many more shall come thereafter

but these are my little contributions to the pot

so, to genuinely believe in you

is to have confidence in your higher self

for there is always

greater greatnesses to be achieved

it is all finally beginning to make greater sense

only a consciously conscientious being

would deliberately choose

to be a part of such a detested vessel

for great challenges are opportunities

to bring out the very best

this way there is much more to be proven

but the scales from our eyes

we must simply remove

for a speck of dust can debar clear vision

so, rinse your eyes by seeking the waters of truth

be not afraid to question all things

for by such

validity has to make itself approved

that the answer has always been within you

for the answer is you

be subjected to nothing or no one

or you'll forever be at its/his or her mercy

the quest has always been

to purify your being internally out

this is the gift that was freely given to all

  — SELF

getting older is only concerned about age because it is a numbers thing. but growing up is a mental thing in that it has little regard for numbers because it has always been without age.

   — tevin dubé

MARSEILLE
The Delaplaine
2021 Long Weekend Guide

Andrew Delaplaine

**NO BUSINESS HAS PAID A SINGLE PENNY OR GIVEN _ANYTHING_
TO BE INCLUDED IN THIS BOOK.**

GET 3 FREE NOVELS
Like political thrillers?
See next page to download for 3 FREE page-turning
novels—no strings attached.

Senior Editors - *Renee & Sophie Delaplaine*
Senior Writer - **James Cubby**

Gramercy Park Press
New York London Paris

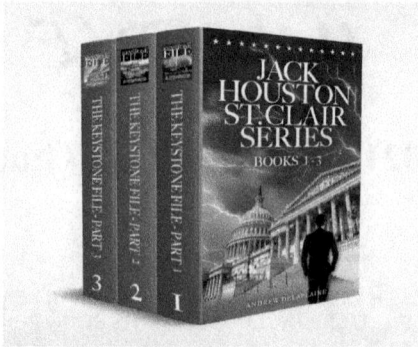

WANT 3 FREE THRILLERS?

Why, of course you do!

If you like these writers--
Vince Flynn, Brad Thor, Tom Clancy, James Patterson,
David Baldacci, John Grisham, Brad Meltzer, Daniel
Silva, Don DeLillo
And - If you like these TV series –
House of Cards, Scandal, West Wing, The Good Wife,
Madam Secretary, Designated Survivor

You'll love the **unputdownable** series about
Jack Houston St. Clair, with political intrigue, romance,
suspense.

Besides writing travel books, I've written political thrillers for
many years that have delighted hundreds of thousands of
readers. I want to introduce you to my work!
Send me an email and I'll send you a link where you can
download the first 3 books in my bestselling series, absolutely
FREE.

Just tell me you're responding to my offer in this book.